Cross-Pollination

By Jennifer Boothroyd

first step nonfiction

Lerner Publications · Minneapolis

LERNER

e

SOURCE

Expand learning beyond the printed book. Download free, complementary educational resources for this book from our website, www.lerneresource.com.

The images in this book are used with the permission of: © BBBar/Alamy, p. 4; © iStockphoto. com/boryak, p. 5; © iStockphoto.com/China500Culture, p. 6; © Ingram Publishing/Thinkstock, p. 7; © iStockphoto.com/yangchao, p. 8; © iStockphoto.com/Shoemcfly, p. 9; © klauspeters/iStock/ Thinkstock, p. 10; © ImageBROKER/Alamy, p. 11; © Max Allen/Alamy, p. 12; © Merlin D. Tuttle/ Science Source, p. 13; © Tim Gainey/Alamy, p. 14; © iStockphoto.com/cglade, p. 15; © iStockphoto. com/aydinmutlu, p. 16; © iStockphoto.com/PhotoRx, p. 17; © Merlin Tuttle/Science Source/ Getty Images, p. 18; © Tom Uhlman/Alamy, p. 19; © Eurpoean Pressphoto Agency/Alamy, p. 20; © iStockphoto.com/jeridu, p. 21; © Gail Shumway/The Image Bank/Getty Images, p. 22. Front cover: © iStockphoto.com/schnuddel.

Main body text set in ITC Avant Garde Gothic Std Medium 21/25. Typeface provided by Adobe Systems.

Lerner Publications Company
A division of Lerner Publishing Group, Inc.
241 First Avenue North
Minneapolis, MN 55401 USA

For reading levels and more information, look up this title at www.lernerbooks.com.

Library of Congress Cataloging-in-Publication Data

Boothroyd, Jennifer, 1972–
    Cross-pollination / by Jennifer Boothroyd.
        pages   cm. — (First step nonfiction. Pollination)
    Includes index.
    ISBN 978-1-4677-5737-9 (lib. bdg. : alk. paper) — ISBN 978-1-4677-6067-6 (pbk.) — ISBN 978-1-4677-6224-3 (EB pdf)
    1. Pollination—Juvenile literature. I. Title. II. Series: First step nonfiction. Pollination.
QK926.R36 2015
576.8'75—dc23   2014015879

Manufactured in the United States of America
1 – CG – 12/31/14

Table of Contents

Making Seeds

Look at this plant. This
flower will soon be pollinated.

Pollen is a powder.

Pollen will be taken from a flower.

The pollen will be dropped
into a different flower.

Plants need pollen from plants like themselves.

The new pollen will help
the flower to make seeds.

This is called **cross-pollination**.

Pollinators

Plants need help to move pollen. A **pollinator** carries
pollen between flowers.

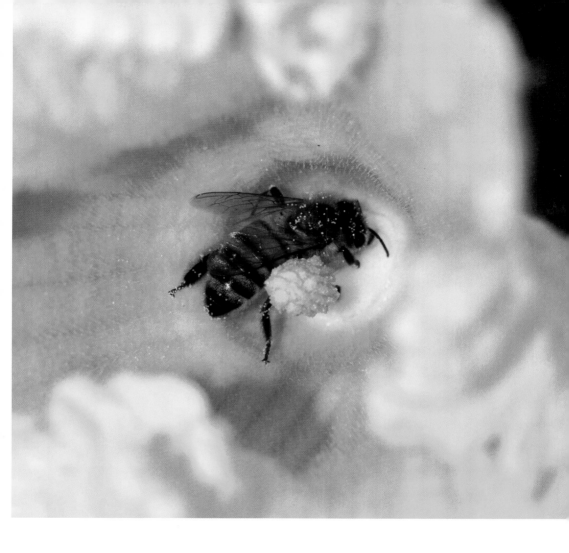

Some insects are pollinators.

Pollen sticks
to feathers.

Some birds are pollinators.

Pollen
sticks to fur.

Other animals are
pollinators too.

Wind blows pollen.

Wind is a pollinator.

Plants **attract** pollinators in different ways.

The smell of tree blossoms attracts bees.

The **nectar** of flowers
attracts butterflies.

Cactus flowers bloom at night.
The flowers attract bats.

The shape of trumpet flowers attracts hummingbirds.

Helping Pollinators

Pollinators help plants. But pollinators need help too. Plants can help pollinators.

Plants make food for pollinators to eat.

Plants hold water for
pollinators to drink.

Glossary

attract – to make someone or something interested

cross-pollination – the movement of pollen from one flower to another flower

nectar – a sweet liquid made by flowers

pollen – a yellowish powder made inside flowers

pollinator – something that moves pollen from one flower to another flower

Index